The Ultimate Cookbook for the Holidays

Amazing Recipes Perfect for Annual Festivities

BY: SOPHIA FREEMAN

Liability

This publication is meant as an informational tool. The individual purchaser accepts all liability if damages occur because of following the directions or guidelines set out in this publication. The Author bears no responsibility for reparations caused by the misuse or misinterpretation of the content.

Copyright

The content of this publication is solely for entertainment purposes and is meant to be purchased by one individual. Permission is not given to any individual who copies, sells or distributes parts or the whole of this publication unless it is explicitly given by the Author in writing.

Table of Contents

Introduction

No holiday celebration would be complete without a grand food feast, right?

Most people agree.

But here's one thing everyone should remember: just because it's the holiday season, it doesn't mean that you should forget all about your health.

The holidays do not give you a free pass to unhealthy dishes.

The fact is, you can enjoy the festivities without ruining your diet or putting your health at risk.

How is this possible?

This book will answer this question with its collection of amazingly delicious recipes that are healthy and nutritious at the same time.

Not only that, but most of these recipes are also a cinch to make, requiring only a few minutes of active preparation.

Some people spend long hours inside the kitchen preparing delicious but elaborate meals that when dinnertime comes, they are already too tired to join the celebration.

Don't let this happen.

Aside from great food, your family and friends want to spend time with you too.

Let these recipes make sure that you get to serve amazing food feast for your loved ones and at the same time, enjoy the festivities with them.

Pepper Glazed Ham

Serving ham during holidays is a tradition for many families around the world. Here's an easy way to do it. To make this recipe, it's best to use fresh meat that has not yet been smoked or cured to get the best result. Discard the skin but leave a little fat for self-basting while roasting.

Serving Size: 12

Preparation Cooking Time: 3 days and 5 hours

Ingredients:

For Brining

- 2 cups brown sugar
- 1 cup salt
- 6 quarts water
- 4 bay leaves
- 12 allspice berries
- 12 whole cloves
- 2 cups ice cubes
- 10 lb. fresh ham

For Roasting

- Salt to taste
- 5 cloves garlic, crushed and minced
- 3 tablespoon thyme, minced
- ½ teaspoon red pepper flakes
- 2 tablespoons olive oil
- 6 leeks

For Glazing

- 1 tablespoon ginger, grated
- ¼ cup honey
- 1 tablespoon brown sugar
- ½ cup red pepper jelly

Instructions:

1. Add the following brining ingredients to a pot over medium heat: brown sugar, salt, water, bay leaves, allspice and cloves.

2. Simmer while stirring until salt and sugar have dissolved.

3. Pour in the ice and stir.

4. Slice top of the ham with crosshatch pattern.

5. Add this to the brine.

6. Refrigerate for 3 days.

7. When ready to roast, preheat your oven to 450 degrees F.

8. Add the salt, garlic and thyme to a food processor.

9. Pulse until consistency is similar to paste.

10. Add the red pepper flakes and oil. Mix well.

11. Rub the paste all over the ham.

12. Arrange the leeks on a roasting pan.

13. Put the ham on top of the leeks.

14. Roast in the oven for 20 minutes.

15. Make the glaze by adding all the glaze ingredients in a pan over medium heat.

16. Simmer while stirring until the sugar is dissolved.

17. Brush the ham with the glaze.

18. Reduce the oven temperature to 300 degrees F.

19. Roast the ham for 3 hours, brushing with the glaze every 30 minutes.

20. Let the ham rest for 30 minutes before slicing and serving.

Nutrients per Serving:

- Calories 215
- Fat 5.3 g
- Saturated fat 1.5 g
- Carbohydrates 9.1 g
- Fiber 0.1 g
- Protein 31 g
- Cholesterol 88 mg
- Sugars 9 g
- Sodium 536 mg
- Potassium 521 mg

Beet Salad

This isn't like any other salad you've tasted. This one is made with roasted beets, tossed in delicious garlicky dressing and sprinkled with herbs, red onion and walnuts.

Serving Size: 8

Preparation Cooking Time: 3 hours and 15 minutes

Ingredients:

- 1 ½ lb. beets, sliced into cubes
- 6 cloves garlic
- 4 tablespoons olive oil, divided
- Salt to taste
- 1 cup vinegar
- ¼ cup white sugar
- ¼ cup walnuts, toasted and chopped
- ¼ cup onion, chopped
- ¼ cup dill, chopped

Instructions:

1. Preheat your oven to 325 degrees F.

2. Mix the beets and garlic in a baking pan.

3. Toss in half of the olive oil and season with the salt.

4. Cover the pan with foil.

5. Roast for 1 hour.

6. Let cool.

7. In a bowl, mix the sugar and vinegar.

8. Squeeze the garlic into this mixture.

9. Toss the beets in this mixture and marinate for 2 hours.

10. Remove the beets from the mixture.

11. Stir in the remaining oil and the rest of the ingredients.

12. Season with the salt before serving.

Nutrients per Serving:

- Calories 135
- Fat 9.7 g
- Saturated fat 1.1 g
- Carbohydrates 11.1 g
- Fiber 2.2 g
- Protein 3 g
- Cholesterol 10 mg
- Sugars 8 g
- Sodium 150 mg
- Potassium 235 mg

Scalloped Potatoes

Here's a vegan version of scalloped potatoes that your vegan friends will surely appreciate. This is easy to cook, making it perfect during the hectic holiday season.

Serving Size: 10

Preparation Cooking Time: 1 hour

Ingredients:

- ½ teaspoon garlic powder
- Salt and pepper to taste
- 4 tablespoons olive oil, divided
- 1 lb. sweet potatoes, sliced
- 2 lb. potatoes, sliced
- 1 cup onion, chopped
- 3 tablespoons all-purpose flour
- 2 ½ cups almond milk
- ¼ cup almonds, sliced
- ½ teaspoon paprika
- 2 teaspoons fresh thyme, chopped

Instructions:

1. Mix the garlic powder, salt, pepper and half of the oil in a bowl.

2. Toss the sweet potatoes and potatoes in this mixture.

3. Add to a baking pan and roast in the oven at 425 degrees F for 20 minutes.

4. Add the remaining oil to a pan over medium heat.

5. Cook the onion for 5 minutes.

6. Stir in the flour and season with the salt and pepper.

7. Cook for 1 minute.

8. Pour in the almond milk.

9. Scrape browned bits with wooden spoon.

10. Increase the heat and stir until the sauce has thickened.

11. Remove from the stove.

12. Spread the sauce over the potatoes and sweet potatoes.

13. Sprinkle the almonds and paprika on top.

14. Broil for 5 minutes.

15. Top with the thyme before serving.

Nutrients per Serving:

- Calories 199
- Fat 7.6 g
- Saturated fat 0.9 g
- Carbohydrates 29.9 g
- Fiber 4 g
- Protein 3.9 g
- Cholesterol 12 mg
- Sugars 5 g
- Sodium 303 mg
- Potassium 651 mg

Prime Rib

Don't be intimidated with this large piece of meat, it's actually easier to cook than it looks. Most people only cook prime rib during special occasions such as Christmas or New Year's Eve but you can also prepare this during an ordinary night.

Serving Size: 14

Preparation Cooking Time: 13 hours

Ingredients:

- 1 ½ tablespoons garlic, chopped
- 3 tablespoons olive oil
- 1 teaspoon rosemary, chopped
- 1 tablespoon thyme, chopped
- Salt and pepper to taste
- 5 lb. rib beef

Instructions:

1. Line your baking pan with foil.

2. Crush the garlic with a mortar and pestle.

3. Sprinkle with the salt.

4. Mix until it turns into paste.

5. Transfer this to a bowl.

6. Stir in the oil, rosemary, thyme and pepper.

7. Mix well.

8. Rub this paste all over the beef.

9. Add the beef in a baking pan.

10. Cover and refrigerate for 8 hours.

11. When ready to cook, remove the beef from the refrigerator.

12. Let stand for 1 hour at room temperature.

13. Preheat your oven to 275 degrees F.

14. Roast in the oven for 2 hours and 50 minutes.

15. Take it out of the oven. Let rest for another 1 hour before slicing and serving.

Nutrients per Serving:

- Calories 459
- Fat 36.9 g
- Saturated fat 14.4 g
- Carbohydrates 0.5 g
- Fiber 0.1 g
- Protein 29.4 g
- Cholesterol 101 mg
- Sugars 3 g
- Sodium 488 mg
- Potassium 411 mg

Christmas Salad

No festivities are complete without bright, colorful and flavorful salad. Here's one that's perfect for Christmas, New Year's Eve or Thanksgiving.

Serving Size: 6

Preparation Cooking Time: 30 minutes

Ingredients:

- ¼ cup nonfat plain yogurt
- ¼ cup light mayonnaise
- 1 cup grapes, sliced in half
- 1 apple, diced
- ¼ cup dried cranberries
- ¼ cup walnuts, toasted and chopped
- Salt to taste

Instructions:

1. Mix the yogurt and mayonnaise in a bowl.

2. Stir in the grapes, apples, and cranberries.

3. Top with the walnuts and season with the salt.

4. Chill in the refrigerator for at least 15 minutes before serving.

Nutrients per Serving:

- Calories 169
- Fat 10.9 g
- Saturated fat 1.6 g
- Carbohydrates 17.9 g
- Fiber 2.1 g
- Protein 2.3 g
- Cholesterol 5 mg
- Sugars 14 g
- Sodium 125 mg
- Potassium 169 mg

Holiday Casserole

Like salad, the casserole is also a popular item during holiday gatherings and festivities. In this Mediterranean-inspired casserole recipe, we make one that's not only full of flavor and texture but also rich in nutrients so you can enjoy it without guilt.

Serving Size: 8

Preparation Cooking Time: 1 hour and 20 minutes

Ingredients:

- 1 tablespoon olive oil
- 2 cloves garlic, minced
- ½ teaspoon red pepper flakes
- ¾ cup sun-dried tomatoes, chopped
- 1 teaspoon freshly grated lemon zest
- 10 oz. spinach, chopped
- 9 oz. artichoke hearts, trimmed and sliced
- 5 eggs
- 2 cups nonfat milk
- 8 cups whole-wheat bread, sliced
- 1 cup feta cheese, crumbled

Instructions:

1. In a pan over low heat, add the oil, garlic, red pepper, tomatoes and lemon zest.

2. Cook while stirring for 3 minutes.

3. In a bowl, mix the spinach and artichokes.

4. Add the garlic mixture to the spinach bowl.

5. Preheat your oven to 350 degrees F.

6. In another bowl, beat the eggs and stir in the milk.

7. Add the spinach mixture to this bowl.

8. Stir in the bread and feta.

9. Spread the mixture in a baking pan.

10. Let sit for 30 minutes.

11. Bake in the oven for 35 minutes.

12. Let sit for 10 minutes before serving.

Nutrients per Serving:

- Calories 277
- Fat 9.9 g
- Saturated fat 4.5 g
- Carbohydrates 30.5 g
- Fiber 4.8 g
- Protein 14.4 g
- Cholesterol 136 mg
- Sugars 6 g
- Sodium 498 mg
- Potassium 542 mg

Roasted Turkey with Rosemary

Roasted turkey is a staple during Thanksgiving. But once you get a taste of this particular dish, you'd probably be serving roasted turkey during any occasion, and each time you have the chance. What makes it extra special is the infusion of lemon zest, herbs and garlic, plus the homemade creamy gravy.

Serving Size: 8

Preparation Cooking Time: 1 hour and 15 minutes

Ingredients:

Turkey

- 1 shallot, minced
- 6 cloves garlic, crushed and minced
- 6 tablespoons butter, softened
- 2 tablespoons mustard
- 2 tablespoons fresh rosemary, chopped
- 1 teaspoon salt
- 1 teaspoon lemon zest
- 1 turkey, neck and giblets removed
- 1 onion, sliced into wedges
- 1 celery, chopped
- 1 carrot, sliced
- 1 lemon, sliced in half
- 5 sprigs fresh thyme
- 5 sprigs fresh sage
- 5 sprigs rosemary

Gravy

- ¼ cup pan drippings from turkey
- 2 cloves garlic, crushed and minced
- 1 shallot, minced
- ¼ cup all-purpose flour
- ½ cup dry white wine
- 3 cups reduced-sodium chicken broth
- 1 tablespoon fresh thyme, chopped
- 1 tablespoon fresh sage, chopped
- ¼ cup heavy cream
- Salt and pepper to taste

Instructions:

1. Mix the shallot, garlic, butter, mustard, fresh rosemary, salt and lemon zest in a bowl.

2. Place the turkey in a baking pan.

3. Push the skin to loosen.

4. Rub the garlic butter mixture all over the turkey.

5. Cover the turkey and refrigerate for 4 hours.

6. Take it out of the refrigerator and let stand for 1 hour.

7. Preheat your oven to 450 degrees F.

8. Stuff the turkey cavity with the onion, celery, carrot, lemon, and herb sprigs.

9. Tie the legs with kitchen string.

10. Roast the turkey for 30 minutes.

11. Reduce the oven temperature to 350 degrees F.

12. Wrap the turkey with foil and roast for 2 hours.

13. Take ¼ cup of the drippings from the pan.

14. Let stand for 45 minutes before carving.

15. Prepare the gravy by adding the drippings into a pan over medium heat.

16. Stir in the garlic and shallot and cook for 3 minutes.

17. Add the flour and cook while stirring for 1 minute.

18. Add the wine and cook for another 1 minute.

19. Add the broth, thyme and sage. Cook while stirring for 10 minutes.

20. Stir in the cream, salt and pepper. Cook for 2 minutes.

21. Serve the turkey with the homemade gravy.

Nutrients per Serving:

- Calories 184
- Fat 6.7 g
- Saturated fat 3.2 g
- Carbohydrates 2.1 g
- Fiber 0.1 g
- Protein 26.2 g
- Cholesterol 79 mg
- Sugars 2 g
- Sodium 259 mg
- Potassium 233 mg

Herbed Turkey

This is another turkey recipe that you'd proudly serve to family and friends. After careful roasting, garnish with lemon wedges and herbs to complete the presentation. This will surely be the star of the festivities.

Serving Size: 12

Preparation Cooking Time: 3 hours and 30 minutes

Ingredients:

- 1 turkey
- 2 tablespoons vegetable oil
- ¼ cup mixed fresh herbs, chopped
- Salt and pepper to taste
- 20 sprigs fresh herbs (rosemary, oregano, thyme, marjoram)
- 2 cups oranges, sliced into wedges plus more for garnish
- 3 cups water

Instructions:

1. Preheat your oven to 475 degrees F.

2. Place the turkey in a roasting pan.

3. In a bowl, mix the oil, chopped herbs, salt and pepper.

4. Rub this mixture on all sides of turkey.

5. Add the orange wedges and herb sprigs inside the cavity.

6. Tuck the wings and tie the legs.

7. Add the water to the pan.

8. Roast in the oven for 45 minutes.

9. Cover with foil and continue roasting at 350 degrees F for 1 hour and 15 minutes.

10. Let stand for 20 minutes before carving.

Nutrients per Serving:

- Calories 146
- Fat 4.3 g
- Saturated fat 1 g
- Carbohydrates 0.2 g
- Fiber 0.1 g
- Protein 25 g
- Cholesterol 82 mg
- Sugars 1 g
- Sodium 202 mg
- Potassium 210 mg

Pork Tenderloin with Green Beans

To make pork tenderloin extra special, wrap it with bacon and serve it with green beans topped with slivered almonds on the side.

Serving Size: 4

Preparation Cooking Time: 45 minutes

Ingredients:

- 1 teaspoon red wine vinegar
- ¼ cup cherry preserves
- 1 lb. pork tenderloin
- 10 slices bacon
- 1 tablespoon olive oil
- 8 oz. green beans, trimmed
- 2 tablespoons honey
- ¼ cup low-sodium chicken broth
- Salt to taste
- ¼ cup almonds, slivered and toasted

Instructions:

1. Preheat your oven to 425 degrees F.

2. Line your baking pan with foil.

3. In a bowl, mix the vinegar and cherry preserves. Set aside.

4. Wrap the pork tenderloin with the bacon slices.

5. Add this to the pan and roast for 20 minutes.

6. Brush with the vinegar mixture.

7. Roast for 10 more minutes or until bacon is crispy.

8. In a pan over medium heat, add the oil and cook the green beans for 4 minutes.

9. Stir in the honey, salt and broth.

10. Cook for 3 minutes.

11. Serve the pork tenderloin with the green beans on the side.

12. Top the green beans with the almonds.

Nutrients per Serving:

- Calories 351
- Fat 12 g
- Saturated fat 3 g
- Carbohydrates 28 g
- Fiber 2 g
- Protein 31 g
- Cholesterol 82 mg
- Sugars 20 g
- Sodium 426 mg
- Potassium 341 mg

Pork Roast

Pork roast is one of the dishes that people look forward to during the holiday season. Here's a recipe that lets you cook it without the fuss.

Serving Size: 8

Preparation Cooking Time: 5 hours and 30 minutes

Ingredients:

- 1 beef chuck pot roast (boneless)
- 1 tablespoon olive oil
- 1 onion, chopped
- 1 clove garlic, crushed and minced
- 2 stalks celery, chopped
- 2 carrots, chopped
- 1 bay leaf
- ¾ cup reduced-sodium beef broth
- 2 tablespoons quick-cooking tapioca, crushed
- ¼ cup dry red wine
- 1 teaspoon garlic powder
- 1 tablespoon tomato paste
- 1 tablespoon dried Italian seasoning, crushed
- ½ teaspoon paprika
- ½ teaspoon dry mustard
- Salt and pepper to taste
- 4 cups cooked mashed potatoes

Instructions:

1. In a pan over medium heat, add the oil and once hot, cook the meat until brown on all sides.

2. Remove from the pan and set aside.

3. In a slow cooker, add the onion, garlic, celery, carrots and bay leaf.

4. Mix well.

5. Top this mixture with the meat.

6. In a bowl, mix the rest of the ingredients except the mashed potatoes.

7. Pour this mixture over the meat.

8. Cover the pot.

9. Cook on high setting for 5 hours.

10. Discard the bay leaf.

11. Pour the sauce over the meat and veggies.

12. Serve with the cooked mashed potatoes on the side.

Nutrients per Serving:

- Calories 241
- Fat 7.8 g
- Saturated fat 2.5 g
- Carbohydrates 7.4 g
- Fiber 1.2 g
- Protein 32.4 g
- Cholesterol 62 mg
- Sugars 2 g
- Sodium 204 mg
- Potassium 608 mg

Marinated Veggies

Just because it's the holiday season, it does not mean you can completely forget about healthy eating. But it doesn't mean that you have to deprive yourself of the merrymaking either. Here's recipe that lets you enjoy the festivities without putting your health at risk.

Serving Size: 6

Preparation Cooking Time: 2 hours and 20 minutes

Ingredients:

- 1 ¼ cup mushrooms, sliced
- 1 ½ cup cauliflower florets
- 1 ¼ cup asparagus, trimmed
- ¼ cup olive oil
- 2 cloves garlic, crushed and minced
- Salt and pepper to taste
- 2 sprigs fresh rosemary
- 3 tablespoons red-wine vinegar

Instructions:

1. Boil the mushrooms, cauliflower and asparagus in water for 1 minute.

2. Transfer to a strainer and rinse under cool running water.

3. In a bowl, mix the oil, garlic, salt, pepper, rosemary and vinegar.

4. Marinate the veggies in this mixture.

5. Cover the bowl and refrigerate for 2 hours.

Nutrients per Serving:

- Calories 48
- Fat 3.7 g
- Saturated fat 0.5 g
- Carbohydrates 3.1 g
- Fiber 1.1 g
- Protein 1.5 g
- Cholesterol 10 mg
- Sugars 1 g
- Sodium 85 mg
- Potassium 207 mg

Garlic Rosemary Beef

It's so easy for this dish to become the star of your holiday festivities. Not to mention, it's also easy to prepare and cook even when you're expecting a lot of guests to come over.

Serving Size: 8

Preparation Cooking Time: 1 hour

Ingredients:

- 3 lb. beef roast (boneless)
- Salt and pepper to taste
- 1 tablespoon vegetable oil
- 3 tablespoons butter
- 3 cloves garlic, crushed and minced
- 2 tablespoons rosemary, chopped
- ¼ cup shallot, chopped
- 1 cup nonfat Greek yogurt
- 1 clove garlic, grated
- 1 teaspoon freshly squeezed lemon juice
- 1 teaspoon Dijon mustard
- 1 tablespoon horseradish

Instructions:

1. Preheat your oven to 400 degrees F.

2. Season both sides of the roast with the salt and pepper.

3. Add the oil to a pan over medium heat.

4. Cook the roast until brown on all sides.

5. Remove from the pan and set aside.

6. Mix the butter, minced garlic, rosemary and shallot in a bowl.

7. Transfer the beef to a baking pan.

8. Pour the butter mixture on top of the beef.

9. Roast in the oven for 40 minutes.

10. Let sit for 10 minutes before slicing.

11. Mix the rest of the ingredients in a bowl.

12. Season with the salt and pepper.

13. Slice the beef and serve with the sauce.

Nutrients per Serving:

- Calories 359
- Fat 20.3 g
- Saturated fat 8.4 g
- Carbohydrates 2.4 g
- Fiber 0.2 g
- Protein 39.7 g
- Cholesterol 129 mg
- Sugars 1 g
- Sodium 417 mg
- Potassium 645 mg

Mushrooms Green Beans

Your family and friends will be delighted with this green bean casserole that's made with mushrooms and creamy sauce and topped with crispy shallots.

Serving Size: 10

Preparation Cooking Time: 1 hour and 40 minutes

Ingredients:

- 2 cups sliced shallots, separated into rings and divided
- 6 tablespoons olive oil
- 1 cup mushrooms, sliced
- 4 cloves garlic, sliced
- 1 cup heavy cream
- 4 cups mushroom broth
- 2 lb. green beans, trimmed
- Salt to taste
- 2 tablespoons chives, minced

Instructions:

1. Pour the oil in a pan over medium heat.

2. Once hot, add 1 ½ cups of shallots.

3. Cook for 5 to 7 minutes.

4. Drain on a plate lined with paper towel.

5. Add the mushrooms to the pan and cook for 2 minutes.

6. Add the garlic and remaining shallots.

7. Cook for 1 minute.

8. Stir in the cream and cook for 2 minutes.

9. Pour in the broth and simmer for 30 minutes.

10. Fill another pot with water.

11. Boil the green beans for 2 minutes.

12. Drain the green beans and rinse with cool water.

13. Add the mushroom mixture to a blender.

14. Season with the salt.

15. Blend until smooth.

16. Pour the mixture over the green beans.

17. Top with the chives and fried shallot rings.

Nutrients per Serving:

- Calories 214
- Fat 17.3 g
- Saturated fat 6.8 g
- Carbohydrates 13.1 g
- Fiber 3.6 g
- Protein 3.4 g
- Cholesterol 27 mg
- Sugars 6 g
- Sodium 317 mg
- Potassium 360 mg

Pork Tenderloin with Roasted Cauliflower Potatoes

Like the previous pork tenderloin recipe, this one is also wrapped with bacon. The difference is that for this recipe, you'll be using turkey bacon instead of pork, and serve it with roasted vegetables.

Serving Size: 4

Preparation Cooking Time: 1 hour

Ingredients:

- 2 tablespoons honey
- 2 tablespoons Dijon mustard
- 1 lb. pork tenderloin
- 3 slices turkey bacon
- 6 cups cauliflower florets
- 12 oz. potatoes, sliced into wedges
- Salt and pepper to taste
- 2 tablespoons olive oil
- ¼ cup parsley
- 1 ½ oz. spinach
- 1 clove garlic, minced
- 1 oz. Parmesan cheese, grated
- 1 tablespoon water
- 2 teaspoons freshly squeezed lemon juice

Instructions:

1. Preheat your oven to 425 degrees F.

2. Mix the honey and mustard in a bowl.

3. Take half of it and brush on all sides of pork.

4. Wrap the turkey bacon around the pork.

5. Place this in a baking pan.

6. Place the cauliflower and potatoes around the pork.

7. Pour the remaining mixture over the veggies.

8. Season with the salt and pepper.

9. Roast in the oven for 30 minutes.

10. Add the rest of the ingredients in a food processor.

11. Pulse until smooth.

12. Slice the pork.

13. Serve with the roasted veggies and pesto sauce.

Nutrients per Serving:

- Calories 404
- Fat 17 g
- Saturated fat 4.3 g
- Carbohydrates 32 g
- Fiber 5.2 g
- Protein 33.1 g
- Cholesterol 84 mg
- Sugars 13 g
- Sodium 726 mg
- Potassium 1313 mg

Chicken Grilled Veggies

Everyone will surely be in the mood to party with this beer-glazed chicken dish served with grilled vegetables.

Serving Size: 4

Preparation Cooking Time: 1 hour and 20 minutes

Ingredients:

- ½ teaspoon ground cumin
- 1 tablespoon dried oregano
- 6 cloves garlic, peeled
- ¾ cup beer
- ½ teaspoon red pepper flakes
- 3 tablespoons brown sugar
- 4 chicken legs
- 2 onions, sliced into rounds
- 2 ears corn, sliced in half
- 2 zucchini, sliced
- 2 tablespoons olive oil
- Chopped fresh chives
- Salt and pepper to taste

Instructions:

1. Preheat your grill.

2. Mix the salt, pepper, cumin and oregano in a bowl.

3. In a pan over medium heat, add the garlic, beer, red pepper and brown sugar.

4. Take 1 tablespoon of the cumin mixture and add to the pan.

5. Simmer for 20 minutes.

6. Rub the chicken with the dry spice mixture.

7. Grill the chicken for 7 to 8 minutes per side.

8. Brush with the beer glaze.

9. Grill for 2 minutes.

10. Toss the onions, corn and zucchini in oil.

11. Season with the salt and pepper.

12. Grill for 6 to 7 minutes.

13. Serve the chicken with the grilled veggies.

14. Garnish with the chives.

Nutrients per Serving:

- Calories 467
- Fat 20.7 g
- Saturated fat 4.7 g
- Carbohydrates 32.3 g
- Fiber 3.5 g
- Protein 36 g
- Cholesterol 115 mg
- Sugars 18 g
- Sodium 553 mg
- Potassium 776 mg

Mexican Pasta Salad

Pasta salads are always a big hit during parties and holiday gatherings. Here's a quick pasta salad recipe infused with Mexican flavors.

Serving Size: 1

Preparation Cooking Time: 15 minutes

Ingredients:

- 1 tablespoon Greek yogurt
- 1 tablespoon tomato salsa
- 1 cup tomatoes, chopped
- ¾ cup red bell pepper, chopped
- 4 oz. edamame, cooked
- ½ cup orzo, cooked
- ¼ cup red onion, chopped
- 2 tablespoons pepper Jack cheese, shredded
- Salt and pepper to taste
- Hot sauce
- Lime wedges

Instructions:

1. Combine the yogurt and salsa in a bowl.

2. In another bowl, mix the rest of the ingredients except the salt, pepper, hot sauce and lime.

3. Pour the salsa dressing on top of the veggies and pasta.

4. Toss to coat evenly.

5. Sprinkle with the salt and pepper.

6. Drizzle with the hot sauce.

7. Serve with the lime wedges.

Nutrients per Serving:

- Calories 403
- Fat 13.4 g
- Saturated fat 3.4 g
- Carbohydrates 50.6 g
- Fiber 15.4 g
- Protein 24 g
- Cholesterol 14 mg
- Sugars 14 g
- Sodium 520 mg
- Potassium 1229 mg

Sweet Potato Casserole

This is a classic Thanksgiving dish that people look forward to. Make this in the pressure cooker to hasten the preparations.

Serving Size: 10

Preparation Cooking Time: 40 minutes

Ingredients:

- 1 cup water
- 5 sweet potatoes, cubed
- 1 teaspoon vanilla extract
- 2 tablespoons brown sugar
- 3 tablespoons butter, melted
- ¼ teaspoon ground nutmeg
- ½ teaspoon ground cinnamon
- Salt and pepper to taste
- ½ cup mini marshmallows
- ¼ cup pecans, toasted and chopped

Instructions:

1. Add the water to a pressure cooker.

2. Add the sweet potatoes.

3. Seal and cook at high pressure for 10 minutes.

4. Release the pressure naturally.

5. Drain the sweet potatoes.

6. Put them back to the pressure cooker.

7. Stir in the rest of the ingredients except the marshmallows and pecans.

8. Top with the pecans and marshmallows.

Nutrients per Serving:

- Calories 187
- Fat 5.5 g
- Saturated fat 2.3 g
- Carbohydrates 32.8 g
- Fiber 4.4 g
- Protein 2.5 g
- Cholesterol 9 mg
- Sugars 10 g
- Sodium 194 mg
- Potassium 477 mg

Chicken Nachos

This is a simple and easy nacho recipe that replaces chips with cauliflower so you get to devour on something delicious and healthy this holiday season.

Serving Size: 4

Preparation Cooking Time: 40 minutes

Ingredients:

- Cooking spray
- 3 tablespoons avocado oil
- ¾ teaspoon onion powder
- ¾ teaspoon ground cumin
- ¾ teaspoon chili powder
- Salt to taste
- 8 cups cauliflower florets
- 2 tablespoons onion, chopped
- 1 avocado, diced
- 1 cup tomato, chopped
- 2 tablespoons jalapeño pepper, sliced
- ¼ cup fresh cilantro, chopped
- 2 cups chicken, cooked and shredded
- ¾ cup black beans
- ¾ cup Mexican cheese blend, shredded
- 1 cup cabbage, shredded

Instructions:

1. Preheat your oven to 400 degrees F.

2. Spray your baking pan with oil.

3. In a bowl, mix the oil, onion powder, ground cumin, chili powder and salt.

4. Toss the cauliflower in this mixture.

5. Transfer to the greased pan.

6. Bake for 20 minutes.

7. In another bowl, mix the onion, avocado, tomato, jalapeños and cilantro.

8. Season with the salt. Set aside.

9. Top the roasted cauliflower with the chicken, beans and shredded cheese.

10. Bake for 5 minutes.

11. Top with the cabbage and salsa.

Nutrients per Serving:

- Calories 487
- Fat 28 g
- Saturated fat 6.6 g
- Carbohydrates 27.2 g
- Fiber 11.2 g
- Protein 35.6 g
- Cholesterol 79 mg
- Sugars 7 g
- Sodium 484 mg
- Potassium 1238 mg

Grilled Chicken Wings

Sweet and spicy chicken wings can serve either as appetizer or main course during your next holiday gathering.

Serving Size: 4

Preparation Cooking Time: 45 minutes

Ingredients:

- 2 tablespoons honey, divided
- 1 ½ tablespoons freshly squeezed lemon juice, divided
- Salt and pepper to taste
- 1 tablespoon olive oil
- 1 lb. celery, sliced
- 1 lb. carrots, sliced in half
- 3 lb. chicken wings
- 1 tablespoon butter, melted
- 2 tablespoons harissa paste

Instructions:

1. Preheat your grill.

2. Combine 1 tablespoon honey, 1 tablespoon lemon juice, salt, pepper and oil in a bowl.

3. Toss the celery and carrots in this mixture.

4. Transfer to a baking pan.

5. Grill the chicken for 3 to 4 minutes per side.

6. Grill the vegetables for 10 minutes.

7. Mix the butter, harissa paste, remaining lemon juice, and remaining honey in a bowl.

8. Coat the chicken in this mixture.

9. Serve with the grilled veggies.

Nutrients per Serving:

- Calories 504
- Fat 30.4 g
- Saturated fat 8.9 g
- Carbohydrates 22.3 g
- Fiber 4.5 g
- Protein 33.9 g
- Cholesterol 212 mg
- Sugars 15 g
- Sodium 508 mg
- Potassium 943 mg

Lasagna

When it comes to pasta, lasagna is one of the most popular options during the holiday season. It's special, and requires time and effort to prepare, but it's definitely worth it.

Serving Size: 8

Preparation Cooking Time: 1 hour and 20 minutes

Ingredients:

- 1 onion, chopped
- 2 cloves garlic, crushed and minced
- 1 carrot, chopped
- 12 oz. lean ground beef
- ½ cup water
- 6 oz. tomato paste
- 15 oz. Italian tomato sauce
- Pepper to taste
- 9 lasagna noodles
- 15 oz. reduced-fat cottage cheese
- 1 egg, beaten
- Cooking spray
- 4 oz. mozzarella cheese
- 1 oz. Parmesan cheese, grated

Instructions:

1. In a pan over medium heat, cook the onion, garlic, carrot and ground beef for 8 to 10 minutes.

2. Drain the fat.

3. Stir tomato sauce, tomato paste and pepper in the water.

4. Bring to a boil.

5. Reduce heat and simmer for 10 minutes.

6. Prepare the lasagna according to the directions in the package.

7. Rinse and drain.

8. In a bowl, mix the egg and cottage cheese.

9. Spray your baking pan with oil.

10. Add layers of the lasagna.

11. Spread the cheese mixture and then the beef mixture.

12. Add another layer of lasagna.

13. Spread with the cheese and beef mixture.

14. Repeat layers until all ingredients are used.

15. Top with the mozzarella and Parmesan.

16. Bake in the oven at 375 degrees F for 20 minutes or until the cheese has melted.

Nutrients per Serving:

- Calories 309
- Fat 8.9 g
- Saturated fat 4.8 g
- Carbohydrates 32.9 g
- Fiber 2.9 g
- Protein 25.5 g
- Cholesterol 81 mg
- Sugars 9 g
- Sodium 326 mg
- Potassium 685 mg

Stuffed Mushrooms

Healthy but delicious appetizer stuffed with creamy filling and sprinkled with crunchy topping—for sure, everyone will love this.

Serving Size: 10

Preparation Cooking Time: 40 minutes

Ingredients:

- Cooking spray
- 30 large button mushrooms
- 1 tablespoon olive oil
- Salt and pepper to taste
- 1 tablespoon garlic, minced
- ¼ cup breadcrumbs, divided
- 2 tablespoons parsley, chopped
- 1 tablespoon thyme, chopped
- 4 oz. low-fat cream cheese
- ¼ cup Parmesan cheese, grated and divided

Instructions:

1. Preheat your oven to 400 degrees F.

2. Coat your baking pan with oil.

3. Slice off the mushrooms stems, chop and set aside.

4. Add the mushroom caps to the baking pan.

5. Pour the oil in a pan over medium heat.

6. Cook the chopped mushrooms, salt, pepper and garlic for 6 minutes.

7. Stir in half of the breadcrumbs and cook for 1 minute.

8. Add the parsley, thyme, cream cheese and 2 tablespoons Parmesan.

9. Mix well.

10. Stuff the mixture into the mushrooms caps.

11. Mix the remaining breadcrumbs and remaining Parmesan cheese.

12. Sprinkle this on top of the mushrooms.

13. Spray the mushrooms with oil.

14. Bake in the oven for 20 minutes.

Nutrients per Serving:

- Calories 75
- Fat 4 g
- Saturated fat 2 g
- Carbohydrates 7 g
- Fiber 1 g
- Protein 4 g
- Cholesterol 10 mg
- Sugars 2 g
- Sodium 184 mg
- Potassium 229 mg

Cream Cheese Bites

While guests are waiting for the star of the dinner, you can serve these cute and delicious appetizers—cream cheese crust with cherry pepper topping.

Serving Size: 4

Preparation Cooking Time: 40 minutes

Ingredients:

- 7 oz. refrigerated crust
- ¼ cup cream cheese
- ¼ cup cherry peppers, chopped
- Chopped cilantro

Instructions:

1. Preheat your oven to 450 degrees F.

2. Spray your muffin pan with oil.

3. Spread the pie crust in the kitchen table.

4. Cut into 24 circles using a biscuit cutter.

5. Prick each one with a fork.

6. Bake in the oven for 5 minutes.

7. Spread the cream cheese on top of the crust.

8. Top with the cherry peppers.

9. Bake for 5 minutes.

10. Garnish with the chopped cilantro before serving.

Nutrients per Serving:

- Calories 46
- Fat 3 g
- Saturated fat 1.3 g
- Carbohydrates 4.5 g
- Fiber 0.2 g
- Protein 0.5 g
- Cholesterol 2 mg
- Sugars 1 g
- Sodium 68 mg
- Potassium 9 mg

Goat Cheese Guacamole

Everyone will be so impressed with this appetizer that they won't even think that it only took you 5 minutes to prepare.

Serving Size: 10

Preparation Cooking Time: 5 minutes

Ingredients:

- 3 avocados
- ¼ cup goat cheese, crumbled
- ¼ cup chives, chopped
- 2 tablespoons freshly squeezed lemon juice
- Salt and pepper to taste
- Whole wheat crackers
- Vegetable dippers

Instructions:

1. Mash the avocados in a bowl.

2. Stir in the goat cheese, chives, lemon juice, salt and pepper.

3. Serve with the crackers or vegetable dippers.

Nutrients per Serving:

- Calories 106
- Fat 9.6 g
- Saturated fat 1.7 g
- Carbohydrates 5.6 g
- Fiber 4.2 g
- Protein 1.8 g
- Cholesterol 4 mg
- Sugars 1 g
- Sodium 114 mg
- Potassium 301 mg

Sun Dried Tomato Goat Cheese Bites

These appetizers are ideal for holiday gatherings, when everyone's so busy with a lot of things. These will only take you a few minutes to prepare since you'll be using premade pie crust.

Serving Size: 24

Preparation Cooking Time: 35 minutes

Ingredients:

- Cooking spray
- 1 refrigerate pie crust
- ½ cup goat cheese, crumbled
- ¼ cup sun-dried tomatoes
- Chopped parsley

Instructions:

1. Preheat your oven to 450 degrees F.

2. Spray your muffin pan with oil.

3. Spread the pie crust on your kitchen table.

4. Cut circles from the crust using a cookie cutter.

5. Press the circles into the muffin pan.

6. Bake for 5 minutes.

7. Top each cup with goat cheese and sun-dried tomatoes.

8. Bake for another 5 minutes.

9. Garnish with the chopped parsley before serving.

Nutrients per Serving:

- Calories 48
- Fat 2.9 g
- Saturated fat 1.3 g
- Carbohydrates 2 g
- Fiber 61 g
- Protein 0.9 g
- Cholesterol 2 mg
- Sugars 1 g
- Sodium 61 mg
- Potassium 10 mg

Melon Cheese Board

This appetizer is not just for the tummy, but also for the eyes. Your guests will be very impressed with the mixture of colors, and the overall presentation of this melon and cheese board.

Serving Size: 16

Preparation Cooking Time: 15 minutes

Ingredients:

- 1 ripe cantaloupe, sliced
- 1 ripe watermelon, sliced
- 1 ripe honeydew melon, sliced
- 4 oz. feta cheese, sliced
- 4 oz. Pecorino Romano cheese, sliced
- 4 oz. prosciutto, sliced thinly
- 8 lime wedges
- Fresh basil leaves
- Fresh mint leaves

Instructions:

1. Arrange all the ingredients on a cutting board and serve.

Nutrients per Serving:

- Calories 32
- Fat 2 g
- Saturated fat 1 g
- Carbohydrates 5 g
- Fiber 2 g
- Protein 3 g
- Cholesterol 0 mg
- Sugars 3 g
- Sodium 20 mg
- Potassium 145 mg

Meat Cheese Board

There are too many things to love about cheese boards. From the perspective of the party organizer, topping the list is the fact that this is super easy to prepare. You don't need to do any cooking, but the result is always astounding.

Serving Size: 20

Preparation Cooking Time: 30 minutes

Ingredients:

- 4 oz. pecorino cheese
- 4 oz. Gouda cheese
- 4 oz. Gruyere cheese
- 2 oz. goat cheese
- 2 oz. Gorgonzola cheese
- 4 oz. prosciutto, sliced thinly
- 1 baguette, sliced
- ½ lb. grapes
- 1 cup carrot strips
- ½ cup dried apricots
- ¼ cup almonds
- ½ cup honey
- ¼ cup black or green olives

Instructions:

1. Arrange all the ingredients in a cutting board or serving plate.

2. Serve immediately.

Nutrients per Serving:

- Calories 248
- Fat 12.1 g
- Saturated fat 6.6 g
- Carbohydrates 28.1 g
- Fiber 2.9 g
- Protein 9.5 g
- Cholesterol 26 mg
- Sugars 18 g
- Sodium 374 mg
- Potassium 218 mg

Sausage Bites

These appetizers are so good, you shouldn't be surprised if they're gone in a few minutes. Don't worry, you can make several batches ahead as these are a cinch to prepare.

Serving Size: 32

Preparation Cooking Time: 1 hour and 45 minutes

Ingredients:

- 1 onion, chopped
- ¼ cup apricot preserves
- ½ cup dried apricots, sliced
- 24 oz. chicken sausage links, sliced
- 1 tablespoon water
- 3 tablespoons honey mustard
- ½ teaspoon fresh thyme, chopped

Instructions:

1. Add all the ingredients in a slow cooker.

2. Mix well.

3. Cover the pot and cook on high for 1 hour and 30 minutes.

Nutrients per Serving:

- Calories 69
- Fat 3 g
- Saturated fat 0.6 g
- Carbohydrates 7 g
- Fiber 0.2 g
- Protein 3.4 g
- Cholesterol 15 mg
- Sugars 5 g
- Sodium 217 mg
- Potassium 26 mg

Cheese Fondue

Even those who are not fond of cheese will enjoy this warm and comforting appetizer.

Serving Size: 12

Preparation Cooking Time: 30 minutes

Ingredients:

- 1 ½ tablespoons olive oil
- 1 cup onion, diced
- 2 cups fennel, diced
- 14 oz. canned diced tomatoes
- Salt and pepper to taste
- 3 ½ cups Swiss cheese, shredded
- 2 cups Comte cheese, shredded
- 2 tablespoons all-purpose flour
- 1 teaspoon fennel seeds, crushed
- 1 ¼ cups light white wine

Instructions:

1. Pour boiling water into a fondue pot.

2. In a pan over medium heat, add the oil, onion and fennel.

3. Cook for 10 minutes.

4. Stir in the tomatoes, and season with the salt and pepper.

5. Cook for 3 minutes.

6. Remove from the stove.

7. Add the cheeses, fennel seeds and flour in a bowl.

8. Pour the wine into a pan over medium heat.

9. Stir in the cheese and cook until melted.

10. Add these to the fondue pot.

11. Serve the fennel and onions with the cheese pot.

Nutrients per Serving:

- Calories 202
- Fat 13 g
- Saturated fat 7.1 g
- Carbohydrates 6.3 g
- Fiber 1 g
- Protein 11.1 g
- Cholesterol 37 mg
- Sugars 2 g
- Sodium 175 mg
- Potassium 143 mg

Onion Squash Dip

Make your onion dip creamier and tastier with butternut squash. Serve this dip with crackers or vegetable sticks.

Serving Size: 12

Preparation Cooking Time: 2 hours and 30 minutes

Ingredients:

- 2 tablespoons olive oil
- 2 onions, sliced thinly
- 12 oz. squash puree
- 1 cup sour cream
- 1 tablespoon nutritional yeast
- 1 tablespoon sherry vinegar
- Salt to taste
- Chopped chives

Instructions:

1. Pour the oil into a pan over medium heat.

2. Cook the onions for 20 minutes.

3. Chop and add to a bowl.

4. Mix the rest of the ingredients into the bowl.

5. Refrigerate for 2 hours.

6. Garnish with the chives and serve with the vegetable dippers.

Nutrients per Serving:

- Calories 83
- Fat 5.5 g
- Saturated fat 2 g
- Carbohydrates 7.7 g
- Fiber 1 g
- Protein 1 g
- Cholesterol 9 mg
- Sugars 4 g
- Sodium 156 mg
- Potassium 153 mg

Parmesan Chicken Wings

Here's an example of a healthy way of enjoying the holiday season—cooking fried and crunchy chicken wings without loads of oil. Find out how.

Serving Size: 8

Preparation Cooking Time: 35 minutes

Ingredients:

- Cooking spray
- 2 tablespoons garlic powder
- Pepper to taste
- ½ cup all-purpose flour
- 3 eggs, beaten
- 1 ½ cups panko breadcrumbs
- 1 ¼ cups Parmesan cheese, grated
- 2 lb. chicken wings
- 3 tablespoons balsamic glaze

Instructions:

1. Preheat your oven to 450 degrees F.

2. Line your baking pan with parchment paper.

3. Spray it with oil.

4. In a dish, mix the garlic powder, pepper and flour.

5. In a bowl, beat the eggs.

6. Add the breadcrumbs and cheese in another dish and mix well.

7. Dip the chicken first in the flour mixture, then in the eggs and then in the breadcrumb mixture.

8. Spray with the oil.

9. Place in the baking pan and bake in the oven for 20 to 30 minutes.

10. Drizzle with the balsamic glaze before serving.

Nutrients per Serving:

- Calories 221
- Fat 11.6 g
- Saturated fat 3.9 g
- Carbohydrates 12.4 g
- Fiber 0.4 g
- Protein 16 g
- Cholesterol 122 mg
- Sugars 3 g
- Sodium 242 mg
- Potassium 163 mg

Oyster Gratin

Oysters may not be the first thing on your mind when it comes to party dishes, but you'd be surprised at how this recipe would turn out to be a huge hit among your family and friends. Making them incredibly delicious are the spicy spinach filling and crunchy cheese topping.

Serving Size: 4

Preparation Cooking Time: 45 minutes

Ingredients:

- 12 oysters, rinsed and shucked
- 1 tablespoon olive oil
- 5 oz. baby spinach
- 1 tablespoon butter
- 2 cloves garlic, crushed and minced
- 1 tablespoon chili pepper, chopped
- Pepper to taste
- 2 tablespoons panko breadcrumbs
- ¼ cup Parmesan cheese, grated
- Lemon wedges

Instructions:

1. Preheat your oven to 425 degrees F.

2. Line your baking pan with foil.

3. Arrange the oysters in the baking pan.

4. Pour the oil in a pan over medium heat.

5. Cook the spinach for 1 minute.

6. Drain the spinach in a colander and squeeze out water.

7. Transfer to a cutting board and chop.

8. Add the butter to the pan.

9. Cook the garlic for 30 seconds, stirring frequently.

10. Stir in the chili pepper and spinach.

11. Remove from the stove.

12. In a bowl, mix the pepper, breadcrumbs and Parmesan cheese.

13. Top the oysters with the spinach mixture, and then with the breadcrumb mixture.

14. Bake in the oven for 10 to 15 minutes.

15. Garnish with the lemon wedges and serve.

Nutrients per Serving:

- Calories 122
- Fat 8.4 g
- Saturated fat 3.2 g
- Carbohydrates 6.5 g
- Fiber 1 g
- Protein 4.8 g
- Cholesterol 22 mg
- Sugars 3 g
- Sodium 197 mg
- Potassium 68 mg

Buffalo Cauliflower

When preparing dishes for holiday gatherings, you do have to consider your guests' dietary preferences. To make sure your vegan family members and friends would have something to eat, serve these awesome vegan appetizers—cauliflower in buffalo sauce.

Serving Size: 8

Preparation Cooking Time: 1 hour

Ingredients:

- Cooking spray
- 1 cup almond milk
- 1 cup all-purpose flour
- ½ teaspoon cayenne pepper
- Pepper to taste
- 2 tablespoons onion powder
- 2 tablespoons garlic powder
- 1 cauliflower head, sliced into florets
- 2 cups panko breadcrumbs
- ½ teaspoon garlic powder
- ½ teaspoon onion powder
- 2 tablespoons fresh dill, chopped
- 1 tablespoon cider vinegar
- ¼ cup vegan mayonnaise
- 4 tablespoons Buffalo sauce

Instructions:

1. Preheat your oven to 400 degrees F.

2. Line your baking pan with foil or parchment paper.

3. Spray it with oil.

4. In a bowl, mix the flour, milk, cayenne pepper, pepper, 2 tablespoons onion powder and 2 tablespoons garlic powder.

5. Coat the cauliflower florets in this mixture.

6. In another bowl, add the breadcrumbs.

7. Dip the cauliflower in the breadcrumbs.

8. Place these in the baking pan.

9. Spray with oil.

10. Bake for 40 minutes.

11. In another bowl, mix the remaining garlic powder, onion powder, dill, vinegar and mayonnaise.

12. Drizzle the roasted cauliflower with the buffalo sauce.

13. Serve with the mayo and dill sauce.

Nutrients per Serving:

- Calories 186
- Fat 5.7 g
- Saturated fat 0.7 g
- Carbohydrates 29 g
- Fiber 3.4 g
- Protein 5.4 g
- Cholesterol 10 mg
- Sugars 3 g
- Sodium 341 mg
- Potassium 374 mg

Stuffed Shrimp

Shrimp appetizers are definite crowd pleasers no matter what the occasion is. You'll be surprised at how easy it is to whip up this appetizer recipe.

Serving Size: 8

Preparation Cooking Time: 25 minutes

Ingredients:

- 1 lb. jumbo shrimp, peeled and deveined (tails left intact)
- 6 tablespoons mayonnaise
- ½ cup scallions, chopped
- ¼ cup celery, chopped
- ¼ cup bacon, cooked crispy and chopped
- ¼ cup panko breadcrumbs
- Salt to taste
- Pinch cayenne pepper
- 1 ½ teaspoons freshly squeezed lemon juice

Instructions:

1. Preheat your oven to 375 degrees F.

2. Line your baking pan with foil.

3. Carve the curve of the shrimp but not all the way through.

4. Press to flatten on the baking pan.

5. Combine the rest of the ingredients in a bowl.

6. Stuff each of the shrimp with the mixture.

7. Bake in the oven for 8 to 10 minutes.

Nutrients per Serving:

- Calories 104
- Fat 8.7 g
- Saturated fat 1.5 g
- Carbohydrates 2.6 g
- Fiber 0.5 g
- Protein 3.7 g
- Cholesterol 29 mg
- Sugars 2 g
- Sodium 277 mg
- Potassium 57 mg

Blue Cheese Bites

Not everyone is a fan of blue cheese. But once your family and friends try this recipe and discover for themselves that blue cheese pairs perfectly with fig jam, they'll probably never look at blue cheese the same way again.

Serving Size: 24

Preparation Cooking Time: 35 minutes

Ingredients:

- Cooking spray
- 1 pie crust
- ¼ cup fig jam
- ¼ cup blue cheese, crumbled
- Chopped chives

Instructions:

1. Preheat your oven to 450 degrees F.

2. Spray your muffin pan with oil.

3. Roll out the pie crust on a kitchen surface.

4. Cut out the dough into 24 circles using a cookie cutter.

5. Press each circle into a muffin cup.

6. Bake in the oven for 5 minutes.

7. Spoon the fig jam into each of the crust.

8. Top with the blue cheese.

9. Bake for 5 minutes.

10. Garnish with the chives before serving.

Nutrients per Serving:

- Calories 51
- Fat 2.5 g
- Saturated fat 1.1 g
- Carbohydrates 6.6 g
- Fiber 0.2 g
- Protein 0.6 g
- Cholesterol 1 mg
- Sugars 2 g
- Sodium 51 mg
- Potassium 12 mg

Caprese Skewers

The classic Caprese appetizers made even more attractive with the use of skewers.

Serving Size: 8

Preparation Cooking Time: 40 minutes

Ingredients:

- 2 peaches, pitted and sliced in half
- 1 teaspoon brown sugar
- 24 cherry tomatoes
- 48 mozzarella balls
- 24 slices prosciutto
- 24 basil leaves
- 2 tablespoons balsamic glaze

Instructions:

1. Preheat your grill.

2. Grill the peaches for 2 minutes per side.

3. Sprinkle both sides with the sugar.

4. Let cool and then slice into 24 cubes.

5. Thread the peaches and the rest of the ingredients into the skewers.

6. Drizzle top with the balsamic glaze.

Nutrients per Serving:

- Calories 79
- Fat 4 g
- Saturated fat 2 g
- Carbohydrates 6 g
- Fiber 1 g
- Protein 4 g
- Cholesterol 10 mg
- Sugars 4 g
- Sodium 263 mg
- Potassium 445 mg

Antipasto Skewers

Wow your family and friends with this bright and cheery appetizer that's also a cinch to prepare.

Serving Size: 12

Preparation Cooking Time: 40 minutes

Ingredients:

- 24 cheese-stuffed tortellini
- 2 teaspoons white wine vinegar
- 3 tablespoons olive oil
- 1 teaspoon fresh rosemary leaves, chopped
- 4 to 6 red bell peppers, roasted and sliced into 24 pieces
- 24 basil leaves
- 12 salami slices, sliced in half
- 24 black olives, pitted

Instructions:

1. Prepare the tortellini according to the directions in the package, skipping the salt.

2. In a bowl, mix the vinegar, oil and rosemary.

3. Thread the bell pepper, basil leaves, salami, olives and tortellini into skewers.

4. Drizzle the rosemary mixture on top.

5. Serve right away.

Nutrients per Serving:

- Calories 96
- Fat 7 g
- Saturated fat 2 g
- Carbohydrates 6 g
- Fiber 1 g
- Protein 3 g
- Cholesterol 12 mg
- Sugars 1 g
- Sodium 205 mg
- Potassium 334 mg

Pimiento Balls

These bite-size treats can be a great addition to your holiday menu. It's so easy to make so you don't feel bad at all when guests devour everything in only a few seconds.

Serving Size: 42

Preparation Cooking Time: 1 hour

Ingredients:

- ¼ cup cream cheese
- 2 cups Monterey Jack cheese
- 2 cups cheddar cheese
- 3 tablespoons light mayonnaise
- 3 tablespoons pimientos, drained and chopped
- 1 teaspoon onion, grated
- Pinch garlic powder
- Salt and pepper to taste
- 1 ½ cups pecans, toasted and chopped

Instructions:

1. Blend the cream cheese in your food processor until smooth.

2. Stir in the Monterey Jack cheese and cheddar cheese. Mix well.

3. Add the rest of the ingredients except the pecans.

4. Pulse until fully combined.

5. Refrigerate the mixture for 30 minutes.

6. Form balls from the mixture.

7. Coat with the chopped pecans.

8. Serve chilled.

Nutrients per Serving:

- Calories 66
- Fat 5.8 g
- Saturated fat 2.4 g
- Carbohydrates 1 g
- Fiber 0.3 g
- Protein 3.1 g
- Cholesterol 12 mg
- Sugars 1 g
- Sodium 84 mg
- Potassium 19 mg

Caramelized Brie Cheese

This isn't like any other appetizer you've tasted or served in the past. But for sure, this will make your holiday celebration a lot more memorable. You'll love this Brie cheese poured with caramel sauce and topped with chopped walnuts and pecans.

Serving Size: 10

Preparation Cooking Time: 15 minutes

Ingredients:

- Salt to taste
- ⅛ teaspoon ground nutmeg
- ½ teaspoon ground cinnamon
- ⅛ teaspoon ground ginger
- ⅛ teaspoon ground cloves
- 1 ½ tablespoons water
- ¼ cup white sugar
- ¼ cup heavy cream
- 1 sprig fresh rosemary
- 2 teaspoons butter
- ¼ cup walnuts, toasted and chopped
- ¼ cup pecans, toasted and chopped
- 8 oz. round Brie cheese

Instructions:

1. Mix the salt, nutmeg, cinnamon, ginger and cloves in a bowl. Set aside.

2. Pour the water into a pan over medium heat.

3. Add the sugar and cook for 5 minutes without stirring.

4. Remove from heat.

5. Stir in the cream and cinnamon mixture.

6. Put the pan back to the stove and stir for 30 seconds.

7. Remove from the stove and stir in the rosemary and butter.

8. Let sit for 5 minutes.

9. Remove the rosemary sprig.

10. Add the walnuts and pecans.

11. Pour on top of the Brie cheese and serve.

Nutrients per Serving:

- Calories 176
- Fat 13.4 g
- Saturated fat 6.8 g
- Carbohydrates 8.7 g
- Fiber 0.5 g
- Protein 6.2 g
- Cholesterol 34 mg
- Sugars 7 g
- Sodium 262 mg
- Potassium 86 mg

Cheesy Crab Wontons

If you're looking for something unique to serve in your upcoming holiday gathering, this is one option that you'll find hard to resist—crabmeat and cheese stuffed wontons cooked golden and crispy.

Serving Size: 12

Preparation Cooking Time: 40 minutes

Ingredients:

- ¼ cup light mayonnaise
- 4 oz. Brie cheese, cubed
- 4 oz. crabmeat
- 2 tablespoons chives, chopped
- 2 tablespoons jalapeño pepper, minced
- Salt and pepper to taste
- 24 wonton wrappers
- Cooking spray

Instructions:

1. Preheat your oven to 350 degrees F.

2. In a large bowl, mix the mayo, Brie cheese, crabmeat, chives, jalapeño pepper, salt and pepper.

3. Place 2 teaspoons of this mixture on top of the wonton wrappers.

4. Fold and secure the edges by moistening with water.

5. Add these to a baking sheet.

6. Spray with oil.

7. Bake for 18 to 20 minutes or until golden.

Nutrients per Serving:

- Calories 121
- Fat 6.7 g
- Saturated fat 2.3 g
- Carbohydrates 9.5 g
- Fiber 0.3 g
- Protein 5.3 g
- Cholesterol 22 mg
- Sugars 3 g
- Sodium 242 mg
- Potassium 57 mg

Deviled Eggs

Love making deviled eggs for parties and gatherings? Here's a different way of preparing this popular appetizer.

Serving Size: 12

Preparation Cooking Time: 45 minutes

Ingredients:

- ¼ teaspoon black peppercorns
- ½ teaspoon dried rosemary, crushed
- ½ teaspoon yellow mustard seeds
- Pinch ground ginger
- ¼ teaspoon paprika
- 6 hard-boiled eggs
- ¼ cup mayonnaise
- Salt to taste
- 1 tablespoon Kalamata olives, pitted and chopped

Instructions:

1. Add the peppercorns, rosemary and mustard seeds in a spice grinder.

2. Grind until powdery.

3. Stir in the ginger and paprika.

4. Peel the eggs and slice in half.

5. Scoop out the yolks and mash in a bowl.

6. Stir 1 ½ teaspoons of the spice blend, mayonnaise, salt and olives into the yolks.

7. Mix well.

8. Scoop the mixture on top of the egg whites.

9. Sprinkle the remaining spice blend on top and serve.

Nutrients per Serving:

- Calories 69
- Fat 5.9 g
- Saturated fat 1.3 g
- Carbohydrates 0.4 g
- Fiber 0.1 g
- Protein 3.2 g
- Cholesterol 95 mg
- Sugars 1 g
- Sodium 110 mg
- Potassium 36 mg

Gingerbread House Cookie

It seems like Christmas won't be complete without the gingerbread house cookie. Here's a simple recipe to follow so you can make this holiday treat without the fuss.

Serving Size: 12

Preparation Cooking Time: 2 hours and 30 minutes

Ingredients:

Cookies

- 1 ½ cups whole-wheat pastry flour
- 1 ½ cups all-purpose flour
- ¼ teaspoon ground cloves
- ½ teaspoon ground cinnamon
- ½ teaspoon ground ginger
- ¾ teaspoon baking soda
- ¼ teaspoon salt
- 1 egg
- 2 tablespoons canola oil
- 4 tablespoons butter
- ½ cup sugar
- ½ cup molasses

Icing

- 1 egg white
- ¼ teaspoon cream of tartar
- 2 cups confectioners' sugar

Instructions:

1. In a bowl, mix the flours, baking soda, ginger, cinnamon, salt and cloves.

2. Set your electric mixer to low speed and beat the egg, oil, butter, sugar and molasses.

3. Add this gradually to the flour mixture.

4. Divide the mixture in half.

5. Put one half on a parchment paper and form into a disk.

6. Create 1/8 inch thick circle from the other half.

7. Place both in a dusted baking pan and freeze for 30 minutes.

8. Preheat your oven to 350 degrees F.

9. Use a gingerbread cookie cutter to make the house shapes (structure and roof) from the dough.

10. Bake the cookies for 10 to 15 minutes.

11. Use your electric mixer to beat the egg white and cream of tartar.

12. Slowly add the confectioners' sugar.

13. Beat on high speed until you see stiff peaks forming.

14. Transfer the icing to a pastry bag.

15. Assemble the cookies into a house and decorate with the icing.

16. Let sit for 1 to 2 hours or until the icing has hardened.

Nutrients per Serving:

- Calories 160
- Fat 3.1 g
- Saturated fat 1.3 g
- Carbohydrates 31.4 g
- Fiber 1.5 g
- Protein 2.2 g
- Cholesterol 11 mg
- Sugars 18 g
- Sodium 76 mg
- Potassium 140 mg

Almond Cream Christmas Treats

Kids and kids at heart would definitely be delighted with these almond cream treats which will only require a few minutes of active prep time.

Serving Size: 48

Preparation Cooking Time: 2 hours and 30 minutes

Ingredients:

- ¼ cup cream cheese
- ½ cup butter
- 1 teaspoon baking powder
- ¼ teaspoon salt
- 8 oz. almond paste
- 1 egg
- 2 ½ cups all-purpose flour
- Colored icing

Instructions:

1. In a bowl, beat the cream cheese and butter using your electric mixer on medium speed.

2. Stir in the baking powder, salt and almond paste.

3. Beat until fully combined.

4. Stir in the egg and flour.

5. Mix well.

6. Divide the dough in half.

7. Cover each with parchment paper and chill in the refrigerator for 2 hours.

8. Preheat your oven to 400 degrees F.

9. Line your cookie pan with parchment paper.

10. Roll out the dough and flatten with the rolling pin.

11. Use Christmas themed cookie cutters to form shapes from the dough.

12. Add the cutouts to the cookie pan.

13. Decorate with colored icing.

14. Bake in the oven for 5 to 8 minutes.

Nutrients per Serving:

- Calories 66
- Fat 3.6 g
- Saturated fat 1.5 g
- Carbohydrates 7.3 g
- Fiber 0.4 g
- Protein 1.4 g
- Cholesterol 6 mg
- Sugars 2 g
- Sodium 40 mg
- Potassium 26 mg

Christmas Pound Cake

Make this the centerpiece of your Christmas table and for sure, everyone will be impressed (and excited to get a bite!).

Serving Size: 16

Preparation Cooking Time: 1 hour and 40 minutes

Ingredients:

- Cooking spray
- ¼ teaspoon salt
- 2 cups all-purpose flour
- ¼ teaspoon baking soda
- ½ teaspoon baking powder
- ½ cup butter
- ¾ cup sugar
- 1 teaspoon vanilla
- 4 egg whites
- 2 oz. white chocolate, melted
- ⅔ cup buttermilk
- ¼ cup dried cranberries
- 1 cup fresh cranberries
- 2 tablespoons brown sugar
- ¼ cup freshly squeezed orange juice
- 2 oranges, sliced into sections
- 1 kiwifruit, chopped

Instructions:

1. Preheat your oven to 325 degrees F.

2. Spray your cake tube pan with oil.

3. In a bowl, mix the salt, flour, baking soda and baking powder.

4. In another bowl, beat the butter and sugar using an electric mixer set on medium speed.

5. Beat until fluffy.

6. Stir in the vanilla and egg whites.

7. Add the white chocolate.

8. Mix well.

9. Add the buttermilk and flour to the butter mixture.

10. Beat until fully combined.

11. Pour the batter into the cake pan.

12. Bake for 35 minutes.

13. Invert and let cool.

14. In a pan over medium heat, cook the cranberries, brown sugar and orange juice.

15. Bring to a boil.

16. Reduce heat and simmer for 5 minutes.

17. Add the oranges and kiwifruit.

18. Remove from heat.

19. Slice the cake and add the fruits before serving.

Nutrients per Serving:

- Calories 205
- Fat 7 g
- Saturated fat 2 g
- Carbohydrates 31 g
- Fiber 1 g
- Protein 3 g
- Cholesterol 1 mg
- Sugars 18 g
- Sodium 93 mg
- Potassium 431 mg

Chocolate Peppermint Cupcakes

Show off your baking prowess with these amazing chocolate and peppermint cupcakes that are sure to delight everyone coming to your holiday bash.

Serving Size: 16

Preparation Cooking Time: 1 hour and 30 minutes

Ingredients:

Cupcakes

- 1 ¼ cups all-purpose flour
- 1 ½ teaspoons baking powder
- ½ cup cocoa powder
- ¼ teaspoon salt
- ¼ cup butter
- ¼ cup vegetable oil spread
- 2 eggs
- ½ teaspoon peppermint extract
- ¾ cup nonfat milk
- ¼ cup mini chocolate pieces

Frosting

- ⅓ cup mini chocolate pieces
- 1 tablespoon nonfat milk
- 1 ½ cups frozen whipped dessert topping
- Peppermint Bark
- 2 oz. dark chocolate, chopped
- 1 oz. peppermint candies, crushed

Instructions:

1. Line muffin caps with baking cups.

2. In a bowl, mix the flour, baking powder, cocoa and salt.

3. Preheat your oven to 375 degrees F.

4. Beat the butter and vegetable oil spread using an electric mixer on medium speed for 30 seconds.

5. Add the sugar gradually, continuously beating until fully combined.

6. Add the egg and peppermint extract.

7. Add the flour mixture and milk to the butter mixture.

8. Beat on low speed for 2 minutes.

9. Add the chocolate pieces.

10. Pour the batter into the muffin cups.

11. Bake for 15 minutes.

12. Let cool.

13. Microwave the chocolate pieces until melted.

14. Stir in the milk and whipping dessert topping.

15. Microwave the dark chocolate pieces until melted.

16. Spread on a sheet of parchment paper to create round shapes.

17. Sprinkle with the crushed candies.

18. Let sit until hardened.

19. Break it up.

20. Use the frosting and peppermint bark to decorate the cupcakes.

Nutrients per Serving:

- Calories 202
- Fat 8.7 g
- Saturated fat 4.7 g
- Carbohydrates 27.1 g
- Fiber 0.2 g
- Protein 3.3 g
- Cholesterol 8 mg
- Sugars 16 g
- Sodium 122 mg
- Potassium 44 mg

Chocolate Peanut Butter Truffles

In this vegan dessert recipe, we replace heavy cream with a mixture of coconut milk and peanut butter. The result is surely satisfying for your sweet tooth.

Serving Size: 8

Preparation Cooking Time: 2 hours and 30 minutes

Ingredients:

Ganache

- 1 cup chocolate chips, chopped
- ¾ cup coconut milk
- 6 tablespoons peanut butter powder

Coating

- 2 ½ cups chocolate chips, divided
- Flaky salt

Instructions:

1. Line your baking pan with parchment paper.

2. Add 1 cup chocolate in a bowl.

3. Pour the coconut milk into a pan over medium heat.

4. Heat until the edges start to bubble.

5. Transfer this to the bowl with chocolate.

6. Let stand for 4 minutes.

7. Stir until fully combined.

8. Stir in the peanut butter powder and mix well.

9. Cover the bowl and refrigerate for 1 hour and 30 minutes.

10. Take the bowl out of the refrigerator.

11. Shape into 18 balls and place on a baking sheet.

12. Microwave the chocolate chips until melted.

13. Drizzle chocolate on top of the balls.

14. Sprinkle the balls with flaky salt before serving.

Nutrients per Serving:

- Calories 151
- Fat 11.8 g
- Saturated fat 7.6 g
- Carbohydrates 15 g
- Fiber 3.4 g
- Protein 3.2 g
- Cholesterol 4 mg
- Sugars 10 g
- Sodium 17 mg
- Potassium 21 mg

Chocolate Oranges

Oranges dipped in chocolate are a quick and easy dessert idea that kids and adults will both love.

Serving Size: 30

Preparation Cooking Time: 45 minutes

Ingredients:

- ½ cup chocolate chips
- 4 oranges, sliced into sections
- 1 tablespoon crystallized ginger, chopped

Instructions:

1. Line your baking pan with wax paper.

2. Microwave the chocolate chips for 1 minute or until melted.

3. Dip half of the orange sections into the chocolate.

4. Put them back to the baking pan.

5. Sprinkle with the crystallized ginger.

6. Chill in the refrigerator for 30 minutes.

Nutrients per Serving:

- Calories 18
- Fat 0.9 g
- Saturated fat 0.5 g
- Carbohydrates 3.2 g
- Fiber 0.4 g
- Protein 0.2 g
- Cholesterol 10 mg
- Sugars 2 g
- Sodium 41 mg
- Potassium 17 mg

Star Cookies

Give your guests a treat (without the guilt) with these healthy star cookies made with honey, whole-wheat flour and freshly grated lemon zest.

Serving Size: 36

Preparation Cooking Time: 2 hours and 45 minutes

Ingredients:

Sugar decoration

- ½ cup sparkling sugar
- Red food dye (natural)
- Green food dye (natural)

Dough

- ⅔ cup whole-wheat flour
- 2 cups all-purpose flour
- 4 tablespoons butter
- ¼ teaspoon salt
- 1 ½ teaspoons baking powder
- ⅓ cup corn oil
- ½ cup granulated sugar
- 1 egg
- 2 teaspoons lemon zest
- ¼ cup honey
- 2 ½ teaspoons vanilla extract
- ½ teaspoon almond extract
- 1 tablespoon granulated sugar
- 1 tablespoon honey

Instructions:

1. Divide the sparkling sugar into 2 bowls.

2. Add the red dye to the first bowl, and the green to the second.

3. Mix well.

4. Spread a thin layer of the sugars on a baking sheet lined with parchment paper.

5. Preheat the oven to 350 degrees F for 2 minutes.

6. Turn it off.

7. Place the sugars in the oven and let sit for 1 hour.

8. Prepare the cookie dough by mixing the flours, salt and baking powder in a bowl.

9. Using an electric mixer on medium speed, combine the following: butter, oil, ½ cup granulated sugar, egg, lemon zest, honey, vanilla extract and almond extract.

10. Gradually add the flour mixture to this mixture.

11. Beat until fully combined.

12. Cover and refrigerate the dough for 30 minutes.

13. Take the dough out of the refrigerator and roll out into the kitchen table.

14. Shape into cookies using a star cookie cutter.

15. Preheat your oven to 350 degrees F.

16. Sprinkle the top of the cookies with the colored sugar.

17. Bake in the oven for 12 minutes.

18. Let cool for 5 minutes before serving.

Nutrients per Serving:

- Calories 97
- Fat 3.6 g
- Saturated fat 1 g
- Carbohydrates 15.3 g
- Fiber 0.4 g
- Protein 1.2 g
- Cholesterol 9 mg
- Sugars 8 g
- Sodium 39 mg
- Potassium 16 mg

Berry Jellies

Fruit candies made with cranberry and raspberry flavors are a good addition to your lineup of desserts and sweet treats for this holiday season.

Serving Size: 64

Preparation Cooking Time: 12 hours and 30 minutes

Ingredients:

- Cooking spray
- 2 cups cranberry juice, divided
- 6 packets unflavored gelatin
- 2 cups cranberries
- 3 cups raspberries
- 3 cups granulated sugar
- 2 tablespoons lemon juice
- 2 teaspoons lemon zest

Instructions:

1. Spray your baking pan with oil.

2. Add ½ cup cranberry juice to a bowl.

3. Sprinkle with the gelatin and stir.

4. In a pan over medium heat, mix the rest of the ingredients.

5. Bring to a boil.

6. Reduce heat and simmer for 25 minutes.

7. Pour the gelatin mixture into the pan.

8. Remove from heat and strain into a sieve.

9. Transfer the jelly to the baking pan.

10. Refrigerate for 4 hours.

11. Slice and serve.

Nutrients per Serving:

- Calories 71
- Fat 0.1 g
- Saturated fat 0 g
- Carbohydrates 17.8 g
- Fiber 1.1 g
- Protein 0.6 g
- Cholesterol 10 mg
- Sugars 16 g
- Sodium 2 mg
- Potassium 29 mg

Oatmeal Peanut Butter Cookies

These classic oatmeal cookies won't get out shadowed even when you serve other decadent desserts.

Serving Size: 42

Preparation Cooking Time: 9 hours

Ingredients:

- 12 tablespoons butter
- 1 cup natural peanut butter
- ¾ cup brown sugar
- 2 eggs
- 1 ½ teaspoons vanilla extract
- 2 ½ cups rolled oats
- 1 cup oat flour
- ¾ teaspoon ground cinnamon
- ¾ teaspoon baking soda
- ½ teaspoon salt
- 10 oz. dates, pitted and chopped

Instructions:

1. In a bowl, beat the butter, brown sugar and peanut butter until creamy.

2. Stir in the vanilla and eggs.

3. Add the flour, oats, baking soda, salt and cinnamon.

4. Fold in the dates.

5. Mix well.

6. Cover and refrigerate for 8 hours.

7. Preheat your oven 375 degrees F.

8. Create small balls from the mixture.

9. Press to flatten into cookies.

10. Bake the cookies for 10 minutes.

11. Let cool for 10 minutes before serving.

Nutrients per Serving:

- Calories 133
- Fat 7.2 g
- Saturated fat 2.7 g
- Carbohydrates 14.9 g
- Fiber 1.5 g
- Protein 2.7 g
- Cholesterol 18 mg
- Sugars 9 g
- Sodium 75 mg
- Potassium 82 mg

Gingerbread Cookies

Make these adorable gingerbread cookies for your next holiday gathering. You can even make a vegan version of this recipe by swapping egg with egg product and using dairy-free milk.

Serving Size: 50

Preparation Cooking Time: 2 hours and 30 minutes

Ingredients:

- 1 teaspoon baking soda
- 2 teaspoons ground cinnamon
- 1 cup all-purpose flour
- 1 cup whole-wheat flour
- 2 teaspoons baking powder
- 2 teaspoons ground ginger
- ¼ teaspoon salt
- ½ teaspoon ground nutmeg
- ½ cup sugar
- ½ cup coconut oil
- 1 teaspoon vanilla extract
- ½ cup molasses
- ¼ cup water
- White icing

Instructions:

1. In a bowl, mix the flours, baking soda, baking powder, ginger, cinnamon, salt and nutmeg.

2. Use an electric mixer to beat the sugar and coconut oil.

3. Beat in the vanilla, molasses and water.

4. Slowly add the flour mixture into the coconut oil mixture.

5. Beat until fully combined.

6. Divide the dough into 3.

7. Cover each one with parchment paper and refrigerate for 30 minutes.

8. When ready to bake, preheat your oven to 350 degrees F.

9. Line your baking pan with parchment paper.

10. Roll out the dough and flatten with a rolling pin.

11. Create cookies using a cookie cutter.

12. Bake in the oven for 10 minutes.

13. Let cool for 5 minutes.

14. Decorate the cookies with icing.

Nutrients per Serving:

- Calories 55
- Fat 2.2 g
- Saturated fat 1.8 g
- Carbohydrates 8.3 g
- Fiber 0.4 g
- Protein 0.6 g
- Cholesterol 10 mg
- Sugars 4 g
- Sodium 58 mg
- Potassium 54 mg

Conclusion

During the holiday season, there is so much to do that you should not focus all your time and energy on preparing dishes for your get-togethers.

Use the recipes from this book to make appetizers, main courses and desserts that are not only delicious and healthy but won't take all your time.

Make sure that you enjoy the festivities as well.

Happy holidays!

Author's Afterthoughts

I want to convey my big thanks to all of my readers who have taken the time to read my book. Readers like you make my work so rewarding and I cherish each and every one of you.

Grateful cannot describe how I feel when I know that someone has chosen my work over all of the choices available online. I hope you enjoyed the book as much as I enjoyed writing it.

Feedback from my readers is how I grow and learn as a chef and an author. Please take the time to let me know your thoughts by leaving a review on Amazon so I and your fellow readers can learn from your experience.

My deepest thanks,

Sophia Freeman

https://sophia.subscribemenow.com/

* * * * ★ ★ ★ ★ ★ ★ * * *